A GUIDE TO … Money

CONTENTS

Written by Kalpana Fitzpat

Collins

1 WHAT IS MONEY?

Introducing money

When was the last time you used money? Maybe you used it to go to the cinema, to buy some clothes or even buy an ice cream?

Money is something we use each day, and it plays an important part in almost every part of our lives. But what is it?

Money can be used in exchange for goods like food or to pay for a service, like having your hair cut.

Money has these characteristics:

- Exchangeable. This means we can use it to swap for something as a form of payment.
- Gives value. Money helps us to measure the value, or importance, of something.
- Acceptable. Everyone agrees on its value, and it should be widely accepted.

When you think of money, you're probably imagining a pile of banknotes, coins, or maybe even bankcards. But money didn't always look like it does today.

The concept of money goes back thousands of years and has a fascinating history.

How money started

Bartering

One of the earliest forms of payment was a trading system called bartering.

Bartering started around 9000 BCE in Egypt and involved people swapping items.

All kinds of items were used for bartering. People would exchange bushels of wheat for yards of wood, cloth for bread, or crafts for silk and perfume.

We don't use bartering today, but it still exists in some form. Do you sometimes swap football cards, treats, or even books with friends? If so, this is bartering, because you are giving them something they want in return for something you want!

Bartering as payment had limitations, though. The system only worked if one person had something the other person wanted and was willing to swap.

Currency

Around 1200 BCE, people started using rare or precious objects to pay for goods, such as food, and services, such as fixing something.

The objects were called "currency", and everyone agreed on the value of them. These items were also desirable or useful, so everyone would want them, making them a perfect form of payment.

Some early examples of currencies are:

Cowrie shells

Have you ever collected shells at the beach? It's not easy to find small, perfect shells. If you find some, do you consider them precious and keep them?

Cowrie shells were used as money in the 14th century throughout Africa, Asia and Europe. They were small, easy to carry and a symbol of **wealth** because they were seen as treasured items.

Quetzal bird feathers

Quetzal birds, found in Guatemala in Central America, have beautiful long green and blue feathers. Historically, the feathers were considered to be valuable because they were difficult to find, making them a perfect form of payment.

The quetzal bird is now the national bird of Guatemala, and the country's modern currency is known as the quetzal to honour the bird.

Bafia potato mashers

The Bafia people in West Africa made potato mashers, which became very popular with local tribes and were used for important trades.

Rai stones

These huge doughnut-shaped stones were used to pay for important things on the Micronesian island of Yap in the Pacific Ocean.

The stones were made in neighbouring islands and the Yapese people used canoes to move the huge stones to Yap.

The biggest known Rai stone is over three metres in diameter – even a strong adult would struggle to move it. Imagine fitting that into your pocket to take to the shops!

The stones are known as Yapese stone money and are still used on the island for traditional payments or gifts between the Yapese population. Like other currencies, they are also considered as a symbol of wealth. The older or bigger the stone, the more precious it is.

Notes and coins

Metal money

People started to move away from currency and instead used metal money. You may have some metal money in your money box. But metal money was not always circular like coins we have today. The first metal money appeared around 1100 BCE. It was first made in China using bronze or copper.

spade money

Early metal money depicted objects like cowrie shells or small spades that might have previously been used as currency. This was much easier than sourcing and carrying the actual objects.

The first coins

The first circular coins were made in Lydia, which is now Turkey, around 600 BCE.

The coins were made from electrum, which is a natural mixture of gold and silver. They were known as the Lydian Stater.

Lydian Stater coin

Paper money

The first form of paper money appeared in China during the Tang Dynasty (618–907 CE). The paper money was made from the bark of a mulberry tree and was authorised with a stamp by the Chinese emperor. It was the first time the value of money was based on the stamp of authority rather than the value of an object. Paper money was easier to carry than objects, so it didn't take long for the idea to catch on.

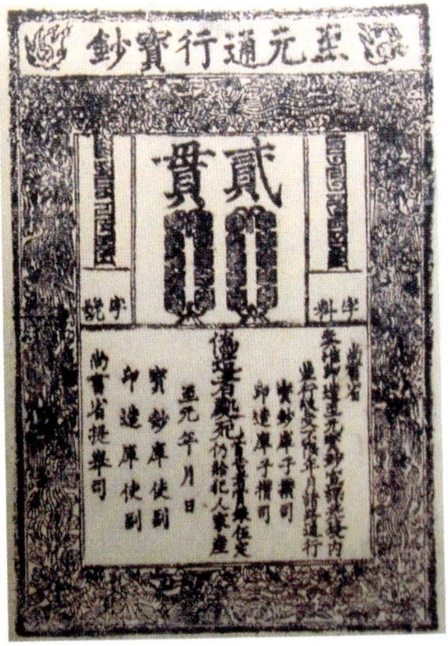

the first paper money from China

Marco Polo

The idea of paper money was introduced in Europe by the explorer, Marco Polo, who travelled to Asia in the 13th century and saw paper money being used. However, it wasn't until 1661 that Stockholms Banco, a bank in Sweden, became the first European bank to print paper money.

Marco Polo

The gold standard

In 1821, the gold standard was introduced, which linked the value of paper money to gold. England was the first country to adopt the gold standard system, but other countries then followed.

Gold was universally liked and trusted around the world. It was also a natural object that was difficult to find, which made it a good **commodity** to determine the value of money. People could exchange their paper money for a fixed amount of gold.

The gold standard was abandoned in Britain in 1931, followed by the USA in 1971, and modern-day money was introduced.

gold bars

Fiat money

The banknotes and coins that we use now are known as fiat money. The word *fiat* is a Latin word. It translates to "let it be done" and suggests authority.

But how can you trust the coins in your money box, and who authorises their value?

Rather than linking with a real item such as gold, each **government** decides how much their money is worth, and it is then used by that country's population. Fiat money is a legal tender, meaning it is recognised by law as a suitable form of payment.

How is money made?

Banknotes

What happens when paper gets wet? It turns to mush! You wouldn't want to take paper money outside if it was raining in case it was ruined, so although banknotes appear as though they are made of paper, they are in fact made from cotton or synthetic materials like polymer to make them last longer.

A central bank oversees printing banknotes. In England, the Bank of England is responsible for printing and distributing banknotes. In the USA, it is the Federal Reserve.

printing hundred-dollar banknotes in the USA

Banknotes and coins often feature characters or images that relate to a country. These could be historical figures, artists or even wildlife. **Euro** banknotes, for example, display windows and doorways to symbolise openness and cooperation.

Banknotes also have special security features like **holograms** or **watermarks**, so that people can't copy them. It's illegal to **forge** money; this is known as counterfeit money.

Coins

Coins are made from metals such as nickel, copper and zinc. The production of coins is known as minting.

the UK Royal Mint producing £1 coins

Coins have an obverse side and a reverse side, sometimes known as heads and tails. The obverse side displays the main design, which is often the head of someone important.

In the US, for example, you may spot George Washington, the first president of the USA, on the obverse side of a coin.

The reverse side of coins may feature images that commemorate special events like the Olympics, important buildings, maps or animals.

a USA coin featuring George Washington

a Japanese 500 yen coin

a South African 5 rand coin

FUN FACT

The world's smallest coin is just 1.99 millimetres in size and weighs just 0.05 grams. It was issued by the Croatian Mint in 2024.

Only 199 of these tiny one-kuna coins were issued.

a 1 kuna coin (actual size)

Global money

Each country has its own money in different shapes, sizes and colours.

As we've already discovered, in ancient history, currency was a term for the precious objects that were used as money, but this word has now evolved to refer to each country's money more generally.

There are around 180 currencies in the world that are recognised as legal tender.

Some countries, like those in the **Eurozone**, share a currency. Twenty of the 27 countries in the European Union use the euro currency. Some countries in the European Union do still have their own currency, though. In Denmark, the currency is Danish krone and in Poland it is the Polish zloty, for example.

Each country's money also has its own symbol to use in writing. Here are some you may recognise. Do you know what the symbol for money is in your country?

If you visit another country, you must get the currency that belongs to the country you are visiting. To get the money, you must exchange it at a currency exchange counter, or it can be ordered online.

Each country's money has a different value, and we use something called an exchange rate to determine how much you would get in the currency you want.

FUN FACT

Thousands of types of coins exist in the world. Some people like to collect them as a hobby.

The largest collection of coins from the same year belongs to Yang Shunfu, from Taiwan, China. Yang collected 80,733 coins! He collected three versions of coins across various countries produced in the same year. His collection put him into the Guinness World Records in April 2023.

2 HOW DO WE USE MONEY?

Uses for money

Money has many uses, but its main one is to buy goods and services. One of the main things we use money for is to pay for household bills. People pay household bills every month with money. But what types of household bills are there?

Energy

Energy bills are important and pay for gas and electricity. We need gas and electricity so that we can use power in our homes. Without electricity you may not be able to watch your favourite movie or play your favourite game, but we also use gas and electricity to keep the house warm in winter or to cook food.

To help reduce the cost of your energy bill, it's important to only use what you need, for example, by switching lights off when they're not in use.

Water

We pay water companies for the clean water we get in our homes – from drinking water to the water to fill your bath.

It uses a lot of energy to clean water, so it's important not to waste it. One way to help is by turning the tap off when you brush your teeth, which can also save money on your water bills.

Broadband

You need broadband to get online, play video games or even watch TV.

Phone

Phones help us to stay in touch with our friends and family. As well as household bills, we also use money for many other important things like buying food, clothing, housing costs or to travel to work or school. All of this is called essential spending.

We can also use money for fun but non-essential things, like buying presents for friends and family or going on an adventure!

What is a bank?

A bank is a place that helps us to look after our money. You can go into a bank to open a bank account, put money in or take money out. Putting money into a bank is a safe way to store your money. Some banks don't have a physical place to visit them, and instead are digital banks where you manage your money using a banking app or online.

Banks play an important role in helping to ensure money is moving around between people and the world.

Access to cash

If we need cash, we can use our bankcard to take money out using an ATM (automated teller machine).

To use this machine, we insert the bankcard into the machine and enter the secret PIN number. The machine will then give the right amount of banknotes needed. We can only withdraw cash if there is enough money in the bank account that is linked to the card.

ATM machines are usually embedded in walls.

FUN FACT

McMurdo Station, Antarctica

The world's southernmost ATM is in Antarctica. There is no bank in Antarctica, and it doesn't even have a currency, but it still has two ATMs located at a research centre called McMurdo Station. Only one ATM is in use and the second one is a backup in case the other one breaks down. The ATM dispenses US dollars.

The ATMs are there for convenience. Although no one lives there due to extreme temperatures, tourists go there and scientists stay there temporarily sometimes, too. They can buy clothes or food at the shops that are mostly found around the research centre.

How do we pay for things?

Physical cash

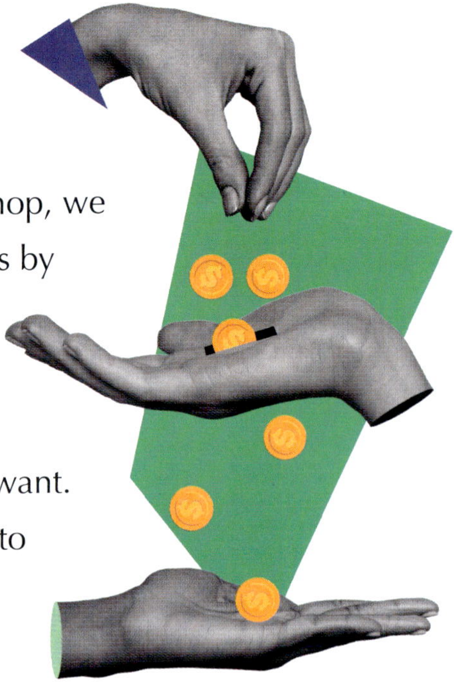

Coins and notes are called physical cash. We can use physical cash to pay for things we need. When we go into a shop, we can see how much something is by looking at the price tag. When we take the item to the cashier, we give them the money to pay for what we want. We can also use physical cash to pay for services like window cleaning, gardening or to fix something in our house.

Using coins and notes has always been popular, but fewer people now use physical cash and instead use digital money.

Digital money

Digital money only exists in an electronic form. It is tracked using computers and linked to a bank account.

Most **transactions** that take place in the world are now made electronically, and only 8% is physical cash.

There are many ways to use digital money to pay for something.

Contactless cards

Most people have plastic bankcards which are contactless. These cards are a popular form of digital money as you can tap them on a machine to pay, which is quick and easy. When we do this, money is taken out of our bank account using **radio frequency identification** or near-field communication technology.

Sometimes, the machine will ask the person to put in a secret code, known as a PIN number, to pay for something. A PIN number is four digits and must never be shared.

We can use a contactless card wherever we see this symbol by tapping the bankcard on the machine.

Smart gadgets

We can also use a smartphone or smartwatch, which also use contactless technology, to pay for things. We do this by connecting our bankcard to our smartphone. We can then just tap the phone to pay in the same way as the contactless bankcard.

Online shopping

Digital money also means we don't always have to go out to buy things. Instead, we can shop online using a computer and a bankcard.

When we shop at an online shop, we enter a card number, the expiry date on the card and a code linked to a bank account to pay.

Borrowing money

Mortgage

As well as looking after our money, a bank also lends money. People usually borrow money so that they can buy very expensive things, like a house. Borrowing money to buy a house is called getting a mortgage. With a mortgage, you agree to pay the money back to the bank in small amounts each month over many years. But when you pay the bank back, you pay back extra money – this is known as interest.

Loan

Some people may use a bank for a loan to help pay for something they don't have money for immediately. A loan allows you to borrow money over a short time.

When you pay a loan back, you also pay interest. A bank will only give someone a loan if it believes the person can pay the money back.

Credit card

Some people borrow money using credit cards. They are like bankcards, but instead of money coming out of your account, you pay a bill at the end of the month for the amount you have spent. You have to be careful to only spend what you can afford, otherwise you have to pay the credit card company a lot of interest. When we owe money to a person or bank, it's known as a debt.

3 MAKE MONEY, SAVE MONEY

Make money

To get money, we must earn it. When we've earned it, we then need to save it to give us **financial security**.

Work for an employer

To earn money, we must work. Work is something we do to share our skills and time and in return we get paid wages or a salary, which is called income. Many people enjoy their jobs. Have you ever been asked what you would like to do when you grow up?

A doctor is employed at a hospital.

Wages can be paid daily, weekly, or monthly and are usually paid into the employee's bank account. Everyone who works gets a payslip to show that they have been paid and how much money they have received.

The company or person you work for is known as your employer.

The money you can earn depends on the **industry** and the level of skills and education needed to do the job. A surgeon, for example, may earn a lot more money than a pizza delivery driver, as the surgeon must study for many years to learn the special skills and knowledge to do their job.

A teacher is employed by a school.

Be an entrepreneur

We don't have to work for an employer to earn money. Some people start their own business and are known as entrepreneurs. When you own a business and it's your main job, it's called being self-employed.

Sometimes it can take a long time to make money from your own business. It can be risky if the business doesn't make enough money to keep it running and pay the owner their salary.

Anyone can have a good business idea.

To help reduce the risk in the early days of setting up a business, some people choose to work for an employer and spend some free time building their own business.

If you have an idea or are good at something, you could start your own business! Although being self-employed is hard work, and it can be risky if your business doesn't make money, many people enjoy being able to make all the decisions about their work. There can also be more flexibility to work at the times you want to.

Save money

When we earn money, it's important to save it, too. This means that once the essential spends have gone out of your bank account, you keep some money back each month and decide how much of it to spend on non-essential things. In the same way, you could save your pocket money or money you receive as a special gift.

Goals

Some people set goals, so they know what they will spend their money on when they've saved it. This could be things such as a holiday, a new car, or maybe even a new house, with a timeframe for when they want to have saved enough money.

Having a goal can motivate you to save. Is there something you think you could save up for? You could set yourself a goal, and a timeframe too.

Rainy day fund

Some people put money away to help pay for any emergencies. This is called a rainy day fund and it's there to prepare for unexpected costs, like a broken window or the car breaking down.

The future

Putting money aside for your future is important and there are many ways to do this.

Pension

Some adults save money into a pension.

Saving money means it can grow over time.

A pension is money you save while you're working. You can then use it when you stop working and aren't earning money anymore, which is known as retirement.

It's important to start a pension when you start working, as it can take a very long time to save enough money for retirement.

Savings account

To save money, you can put it into a savings account with a bank. When you save with a bank, the bank pays you interest to encourage you to save money with them. This means you get a bit of extra money in your savings. Interest is set by a percentage of the total amount you save.

The higher the interest rate, the more money you earn on savings.

For example, if you had 100 coins and the bank paid 5% interest a year, you would have five extra coins, giving you a total of 105 at the end of the year.

Investing

Another way to make money grow is to invest it.

A popular way to invest is to buy shares in companies on the **stock market**. Imagine a big pie. By buying a share in a company, you are buying a small piece of the pie.

When the company you invest with makes a profit, you get some profit too because you helped the company by investing in it.

Investing can be risky, as the value of shares can go down as well as up and investors may feel they need to sell them at a certain point to avoid losing any money.

The stock market can go up and down.

Compound interest

The longer you save or invest, the more your money will grow because of something called compound interest. Compound interest is when you get interest and then receive more interest on the amount you already had, meaning your money can start to grow more.

Let's say you had 100 coins and you earned 10% interest.

By the end of year one, you'd have 110 coins (10% on 100), by the end of year two you'd have 121 coins (10% on 110), by the end of year three you'd have 133 coins (10% on 121). The longer you keep saving, the more your money will benefit from compound interest. By the end of ten years, you could have 259 coins without having added anything extra yourself.

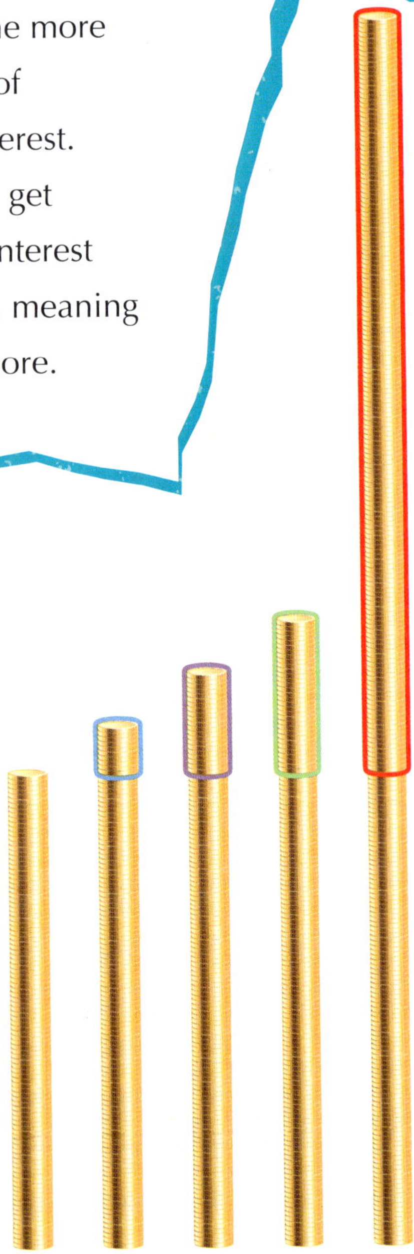

What is cryptocurrency?

Imagine money that only existed virtually … that's what cryptocurrency is. It's money that you can't see or touch. Cryptocurrency transactions are recorded on a **blockchain** and kept secure by **cryptography**.

There are thousands of types of cryptocurrencies. The very first type was bitcoins.

Unlike fiat money, crypto money is not controlled by the government, meaning it is a decentralised currency and it's very risky as its value can rise and fall very fast.

Bitcoins are the most popular form of cryptocurrency.

A money plan

When we earn money, we need a system in place to ensure we have enough money for essential spending and to save for the future. We need a plan in place to help us do this, and this is known as budgeting.

To create a budget, you look at your income, which is money you receive, and your expenses, which is money you spend. It's important you don't spend more than you earn.

Some people use a 50/30/20 budgeting rule. When they get paid, they put 50% of their income towards essential spending like bills and groceries, 30% towards spending on non-essential, fun things, and 20% into savings.

Wants versus needs

When we spend money, it's important to understand the difference between wants and needs.

Needs are essential spending. For example, we need to buy food and we must pay bills like electricity, or we'd have no power.

Wants are things that we'd like to have but don't need. For example, you want a new game, but you don't need it.

Can you see the difference between wants and needs?

We should make sure we have enough money to cover our needs before we spend money on our wants. This is a good way to look after your money.

Charitable giving

We can also use our money to help other people or causes. This is known as giving to charity. A charity can help all sorts of causes, from the environment to animals, or even innovation in health.

You can donate old clothes or shoes that you have grown out of.

You can donate to a charity by giving money to them. Sometimes we donate clothes to charity shops so that they can sell them to raise money.

You can also raise money for a charity by doing something special. Some schools have charity events, like a bake sale, to help raise money.

FUN FACT

Some people have raised money for charity by running marathons and made it into the Guinness World Records.

In 2011, Steve Chalke from the UK made a record for the most money raised by an individual marathon runner, which amounted to over two million pounds.

4 THE ECONOMY

What is the economy?

How people spend and make money is part of the economy.

A country's economy is measured by its Gross Domestic Product (GDP). GDP measures the value of all the goods and services of a country, measured over a certain time, usually a year.

The prices of goods and services change all the time. When prices go up, this is called inflation. It's normal for prices to rise gradually over time, but for the economy to run well, inflation should remain stable and prices should not rise too quickly.

High inflation means everyday goods cost more money.

If inflation rises too fast, it's not good for the country – everything becomes expensive to buy and people won't have enough money for their essential spending.

If prices fall rapidly, this is deflation. Deflation is also not good for the economy as it suggests the country's economy is not growing.

What is a recession?

Sometimes, if a country's economy is in poor condition and its GDP drops, it could fall into recession. If a country goes into a recession, there may be fewer jobs for people and that means fewer people earning money to buy things. A strong economy should have enough supply and demand for the goods that it produces.

Taxes

To help run a country well, the government must provide public services like health support services, education, or street maintenance.

The government collects tax from people to pay for these public services.

What is tax?

When you earn money, some of the money is deducted as a tax payment to the government. Individuals and businesses must pay taxes. In some countries, you also pay tax when you buy goods or services.

If you buy shoes costing 100 coins and tax at 20%, then the shoes will cost you 120 coins.

In many countries, people pay tax when they buy a house or if they make money from savings.

FUN FACT

Tax has been around for thousands of years, and it has applied to some unexpected things.

Urine tax

Roman toilets

In ancient Rome, urine was seen as important because it was used as fertiliser, to clean dirt from clothing or to tan leather. People therefore had to pay tax when they sold urine.

Beard tax

In the 18th century, the Russian emperor placed a tax on people who had beards! The idea was to prevent men from having a beard and instead to be clean-shaven to look more modern. Those who paid the tax had to carry a beard token to prove they had paid.

Imagine if you could create a tax – what would you tax people for?

Money for our future

We all need money to live comfortably. To get money, we must earn it. When we earn money, we must think carefully about how we spend it, making sure we look after essential spending first.

We also need to think carefully about how to save it. By saving our money, we can all have the security of knowing it will be there when we need it – and we can grow it for our future.

GLOSSARY

blockchain a digital record of a purchase, distributed across hundreds of computers

commodity a product that can be bought and sold, such as copper, coffee or gold

cryptography a system of secret computer codes

euro unit of money used by some of the countries in the European Union

Eurozone the euro area that consists of 20 European Union countries that use the euro (€) currency

financial security having enough money to live comfortably and savings for the future

forge to make or imitate a fake copy of something, like money

government a group of people that run the country and are in charge of policies

holograms 3D photographic images

industry a group of companies defined by their business activity, such as healthcare or construction

radio frequency identification wireless communication technology that uses radio waves

stock market organises the buying and selling of stocks and shares

transactions buying and selling things

watermarks designs put on paper which can only be seen when held up to the light

wealth the value of money and possession someone has

INDEX

MONEY CHART

earn money

save money

employed

self-employed

pay taxes

spend money

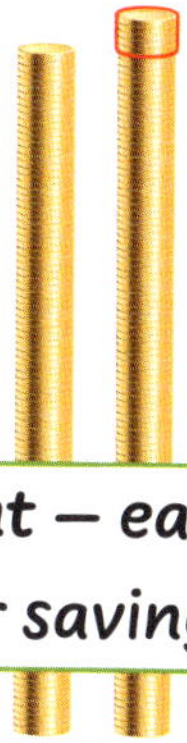

bank account – earn interest to grow your savings

invest – make money grow on the stock market

save for the future

pension

buy a house

go on holiday

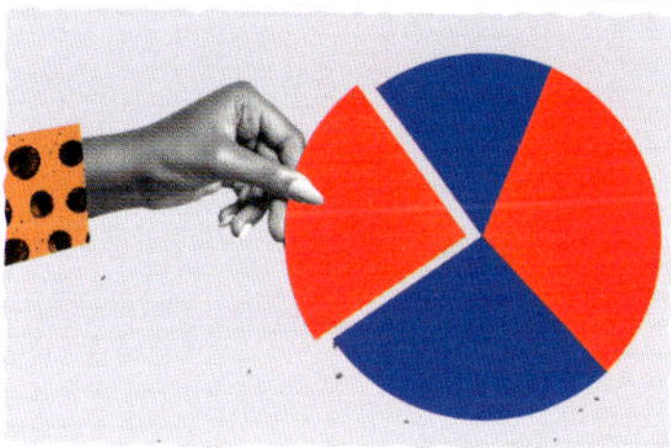

essential spending – needs

non-essential spending – wants

Ideas for reading

Written by Gill Matthews
Primary Literacy Consultant

Reading objectives:

- check that the book makes sense to them, discussing their understanding and exploring the meaning of words in context
- asking questions to improve their understanding
- summarise the main ideas drawn from more than one paragraph, identifying key details that support the main ideas
- retrieve, record and present information from non-fiction

Spoken language objectives:

- ask relevant questions to extend their understanding and knowledge
- use relevant strategies to build their vocabulary
- articulate and justify answers, arguments and opinions

Curriculum links: Geography: geographical skills and fieldwork

Interest words: neighbouring, traditional, considered, symbol, precious

Resources: atlases or globes; sheets of paper printed with 20 boxes

Build a context for reading

- Ask children to read the title of the book and to spend 30 seconds noting down what the word *money* makes them think of. Take feedback, encouraging children to explain why they have noted down certain words.
- Read the back-cover blurb. Point out that this is an information book. Ask children what features they expect it to have and what the purpose of those features are.
- Give them a few minutes to skim the book checking for the features they have mentioned.
- Ask children to look at the title of the first chapter listed in the contents. Discuss the question. Ask children to turn to the first chapter.

Understand and apply reading strategies

- Read pp2–3 aloud. Demonstrate how to summarise the information given on these two pages by identifying the main ideas in each paragraph.